MEETING THE NEEDS OF SPECIAL STUDENTS

SUCCESSFUL SCHOOLS
Guidebooks to Effective Educational Leadership
Fenwick W. English, Series Editor

MEETING THE NEEDS OF SPECIAL STUDENTS

Legal,

Ethical, and

Practical

Ramifications

Lawrence J. Johnson
Anne M. Bauer

CORWIN PRESS, INC.
A Sage Publications Company
Newbury Park, California

For information address:

Corwin Press, Inc.
A Sage Publications Company
2455 Teller Road
Newbury Park, California 91320

SAGE Publications Ltd.
6 Bonhill Street
London EC2A 4PU
United Kingdom

SAGE Publications India Pvt. Ltd.
M-32 Market
Greater Kailash I
New Delhi 110 048 India

Printed in the United States of America

Library of Congress Cataloging-in-Publication Data

Johnson, Lawrence J., 1955–
    Meeting the needs of special students : legal, ethical, and
practical ramifications / Lawrence J. Johnson, Anne M. Bauer.
        p.   cm. — (Successful schools ; v. 6)
    Includes bibliographical references (p.   ).
    ISBN 0-8039-6021-2
    1. Special education—United States. 2. Special education—Law
and legislation—United States.   I. Bauer, Anne M.   II. Title.
III. Series.
LC3981.J65   1992
371.9'0973—dc20   92-4572
                                                    CIP

92 93 94 95   10 9 8 7 6 5 4 3 2 1

Corwin Press Production Editor: Tara S. Mead

Contents

NOTES

Foreword

Many school administrators are defensive and somewhat annoyed with the problems of special education students. The time spent on the students in conferences, in paperwork, in developing the IEPs (Individualized Educational Programs), and with the parents of special education students has left a decidedly negative impression with them about the subject. It has tended to become an emotional shroud that has fostered a quiet but genuine backlash by administrators rarely observed in public but very familiar in battles inside the bureaucracy.

As a former superintendent, I can testify to the negativism and resistance of school administrators to confronting the laws relating to special education, having to equip schools to deal with a variety of exceptional physical conditions, and the disdain felt for "pushy" parents who seem to know all the laws and often bring lawyers with them.

Larry Johnson and Anne Bauer have endeavored to write a book to help administrators become more knowledgeable about the law and about how schools must do all they can not only by virtue of those laws but by virtue of what is *best* for these special students. Their perspective is practical, and they point out what must be done without being shrill or contentious about it. Most of all, this book is filled with helpful hints based on experience with special students in a variety of educational settings in schools.

The school administrator who takes the time to become familiar with the Johnson/Bauer model will feel a lot better about special students and possess confidence that he or she can actually help them.

I predict this book will become a guide for the real problems school administrators face in special education, and it will be one of the more dog-eared volumes in the Successful Schools series. I wish I had had this book to give to some of the principals with whom I worked over the years because I know it would have made a difference to them and to the students in their schools. I would like especially to observe the Northport-East Northport Union Free School District Board of Education that courageously battled the New York State education bureaucracy on behalf of two special education students who had passed their local IEPs but not the state test. I was never more proud to be their superintendent than on that occasion.

As Sarah Lawrence Lightfoot once observed, one of the beacons that displays a good high school is an overriding concern for the most vulnerable students in it. That is a fitting note upon which to begin this volume.

FENWICK W. ENGLISH
University of Kentucky

Preface

More administrators have probably ended up in court due to questions regarding a special education program or student than because of any other situation. Unlike other areas of federal involvement in education, programming for special education students is mandated rather than permissive. Unlike any other group of students, those identified as disabled have a statute defining their rights to free, appropriate, public education. Students who are not identified as disabled have no such guarantee. Unlike many parents of children not identified as disabled, parents of children with special needs are frequently well aware of their rights and those of their children and are used to asserting themselves to protect them.

Administrators, then, must be armed with information regarding the rights of these students. These rights are under the guardianship of the courts; so, in addition to being aware of federal guidelines, administrators must be aware of the case law and precedents regarding these students. And administrators must be aware of the actions, procedures, and strategies that may be employed in their programs and schools to enhance the development of these students and ensure appropriate programs.

It is the purpose of this book to provide this essential information. In the first three chapters, statutes and case law regarding special education students and programming are explored. In the fourth chapter, common challenges confronting the administrator regarding special education are discussed. In the following three chapters, ways to enhance and ensure appropriate educational programming for special education students, as well as all other students, are presented, with emphases on creating opportunities for success for children with special needs, structuring supportive school environments, and working with teachers. The book concludes with a Troubleshooting Guide providing the location of answers to questions that may emerge in practice.

In books such as this one, it is sometimes difficult to avoid the tone of "what you have to do" rather than "what should rightfully be done" to provide opportunities to all children. We recognize the complexity of managing schools, programs, and districts in contemporary society. We also recognize, however, that meeting the needs of 12% of school-aged children cannot be lost in the flood of problems and issues regarding schooling of all children. Rather, we hope the reader views the challenge of meeting the needs of children with disabilities as "what should and must be done."

We appreciate the help and support Fenwick English has provided throughout this project; his focus has been a consistent help. We also are indebted, in particular, to Lou Anne Worthington and Lynn Boyd, who developed the vignettes and participated in the development of intervention strategies contained in Chapter 6. We also appreciate the support of our families throughout the writing process and their patience as we sometimes missed a soccer game or baseball practice so that we could complete this work. And we thank all those special children and their teachers and administrators who constantly remind us that it's all worth it.

LAWRENCE J. JOHNSON
ANNE M. BAUER
University of Cincinnati

NOTES

About the Authors

Lawrence J. Johnson is Associate Professor and Head of the Department of Early Childhood and Special Education at the University of Cincinnati. He is currently the principal evaluator in a national effort to develop training programs to better enable Head Start teachers to address the needs of students with disabilities in their programs. He has developed, implemented, and researched the facilitative collaboration model to support teachers in including learners with special needs in general education classrooms. He serves on the executive boards of the divisions of Early Childhood, Teacher Education, and Research of the Council for Exceptional Children.

Anne M. Bauer is Associate Professor in the Department of Early Childhood and Special Education at the University of Cincinnati, where she is engaged in teacher preparation. Her writing and research topics include classroom structures and behavior management as well as collaboration among teachers and families regarding individuals with disabilities. She is currently engaged in research concerning kindergarten children who are at risk for school failure.

1

Because It's the Law
(and the Right Thing to Do)

A consistently challenging area for school administrators is special education. Due to years of exclusion, the rights of children who need special assistance and their parents are now more thoroughly protected by statute and case law than the rights of all other children. Parents of children in special education programs are often well educated in their rights and serve as strong advocates for their children. To make your life as an administrator easier, it is worth your while not only to be aware of and abide by the laws that protect these children but to structure your school and program to optimize their chances for success.

1.1 What the Law Requires

In 1966, Congress made its first efforts toward providing for special education by adding Title VI to the Elementary and Secondary Education Act and establishing the Bureau for Education of the Handicapped. When Title VI was repealed in 1970, the Education of the Handicapped Act passed, providing grants to states to encourage special education programming. Following a series of cases that set the stage for a constitutional right to special education, because states provide education, Section 502 of the Rehabilitation Act was passed (1973). This act, followed by the Education for All Handicapped Children Act (Public Law 94-142) in 1975, has had a significant impact on how schools work for students with and without disabilities.

1.2 Section 504

Section 504 of the Rehabilitation Act of 1973 requires that "no otherwise qualified individual with handicaps, shall solely by reason of his handicap, be excluded from participation in, be denied the benefits of, or be subjected to discrimination under any program or activity receiving Federal financial assistance." This law made it illegal for any programs receiving federal funding to discriminate against an individual on the basis of handicap. Court cases that emerged from this act indicated that "reasonable accommodation" must be provided to meet the nondiscrimination standard.

Problem 1. A secondary school sophomore with hearing impairment is "trying out" for football. To participate in the huddle, he needs to have a sign language interpreter present. Who provides the interpreter?

Problem 2. The students in the intermediate grades class-room for students with behavioral disorders are difficult to manage during less structured times. Can the principal prohibit the class from attending the school carnival?

Solutions. In both of these situations, reasonable accommodations must be made for the students. The school should provide the sign language interpreter. Efforts should be made to increase supervision of the students with behavioral disorders so that they can participate in the carnival. Both would be considered "reasonable accommodations," and failing to assist the students in participating would be discriminatory.

1.3 Public Law 94-142: Education for All Handicapped Children Act

Public Law 94-142 is a grant statute that creates individual rights. States may receive federal funding to support payment for children with disabilities aged 3 through 21 based on a formula of average per-student expenditures if the state develops a plan for providing for all handicapped children in the state a free, appropriate, public education that emphasizes special education and related services designed to meet their unique needs. The major requirements of PL 94-142 and what they mean for administrators follow:

- *All* children who meet the age eligibility must be provided a free, public education. This assumes that all children are capable of benefiting from education, though the education may include very basic self-help and motor skills rather than reading, writing, and arithmetic. *Therefore the following rules apply:*

If placement in a public or private residential program is necessary to provide special education and related services, the program must be provided at no cost to the parent or child.

Children with disabilities must have the same opportunities available to them as to nondisabled children, such as art, music, vocational education, and industrial arts.

Children with disabilities must have an equal opportunity to participate in nonacademic and extracurricular services.

Physical education must be available to every child.

- This education must take place in the *least restrictive environment; therefore the following rules apply:*

  To the greatest extent appropriate, children with disabilities should be educated with those who do not have disabilities.

  Special classes and schools are only appropriate when the disability is so severe that education in general education is impossible.

  Placements are determined at least annually, based on the IEP, and as close to the child's home as possible.

- This education must be individualized and appropriate to the child's needs. The document used to ensure this individualized planning is the Individualized Educational Program (IEP; specific information regarding IEPs appears in Box 1.1).

- Due process and informed consent are required to ensure that the parents' and children's rights are upheld; *therefore the following rules apply:*

  The parent must be informed of all information relevant to the action for which consent is sought in his or her native language or other mode of communication.

  Parents must be given prior notice if the school proposes to initiate or change the identification, evaluation, or placement of the child or refuses to perform these actions.

  A parent or school may initiate a hearing, which must be conducted by the state educational agency or the public agency directly responsible for the education of the child,

by an impartial hearing officer; any party has a right
to administrative appeal and impartial review.

The child stays in the current educational placement unless the parent and the school agree otherwise.

- Assessment of children must be nondiscriminatory and
multifactored; *therefore the following rules apply:*

Before any placement occurs, a full and individual evaluation of the child's educational needs must be conducted.

Tests and evaluation materials must be in the native language or other appropriate mode of communication,
must be valid, must be administered by a trained individual, must address specific areas of educational need
and not just IQ, and must ensure that the test results
accurately reflect the child's aptitude or achievement.

No single procedure can be used to determine an appropriate educational program.

Evaluation is carried out by a multidisciplinary team.

The child must be assessed in all areas related to the sus-
pected disability.

Parents have a right to obtain an independent educational evaluation of the child at public expense if they
disagree with the evaluation obtained by the agency.

Problem 3. Only one child in your elementary school program is identified as "other health impaired." He requires physical therapy to participate in his educational program. The
parents have offered to pay for the therapy to keep the student
in the regular program.

Solution 3. If the physical therapy is indeed required for participation in the educational program, it must be provided by
the district.

Problem 4. Due to budget cuts, the art and music teachers
are available to your school only twice weekly. To put all of the
regular education classes in the schedule, the special education
classes housed in your building cannot participate.

Q: What goes into an IEP?

A: The five basic parts of an IEP are a description of (a) the child's current level of functioning, (b) goals and objectives, (c) services provided, (d) duration of services, and (e) criteria for evaluation.

Q: Can a child begin special education classes without an IEP?

A: No. The IEP is the placement instrument. Parents, however, must sign an additional consent for placement.

Q: How long after the IEP is written must services begin?

A: There can be no delay in providing services.

Q: Who must be at the IEP meeting?

A: A representative of the school system, other than the child's teacher, who is qualified to provide or supervise the child's program; the child's teacher; one or both parents; the child, where appropriate; and other individuals, at the discretion of the parent or school.

Q: May the IEP be written before the meeting?

A: No. The IEP is collaboratively written by all parties at the meeting.

Q: Is the IEP a binding contract?

A: No. It is a plan for the child's program, and not a legally binding contract.

Q: How long should it take to develop "short-term objectives"?

A: Short-term objectives can usually be completed in three to five months.

Box 1.1. Frequently Asked Questions About IEPs

Solution 4. Students with disabilities are to be afforded the same opportunities as those without handicaps. Find time in the schedule!

Problem 5. A secondary school student's IEP indicated that she would receive speech and language therapy twice weekly. Due to an illness, the speech and language clinician was unavailable for approximately four months. The parents insist that the IEP required the school to provide speech and language therapy and that they will sue the district on behalf of their child for not providing the services and for any loss of the child's skills.

Solution 5. The IEP is not a binding contract. If the school made its best effort to fill the position and provide the service, the parents do not have a case.

1.4 Confidentiality and Privacy

The Family Educational Rights and Privacy Act (FERPA), frequently referred to as the Buckley Amendment, provides protections to parents and children in the areas of access and accuracy of records. Schools must permit parents and students over 18 to have access to their records in certain circumstances. The amendment also protects against unauthorized disclosure of school records. Through this access, the individual can determine whether the information in the records is accurate and complete.

Public Law 94-142 also ensures parents the right to inspect and review all educational records with respect to identification, evaluation, and placement of the child as well as the provision of a free appropriate public education to the child. In addition, a parent who believes that information in education records collected, maintained, or used for these purposes is inaccurate or misleading or violates the privacy or other rights of the child may request that the participating agency amend the information.

Problem 6. A parent requests in writing to see her child's file. The teacher goes through the file before the parent comes to remove information she prefers the parent not see.

Solution 6. Purging files is not appropriate. Files should be maintained in such a way that parents could walk in and review them at any time.

1.5 How Do Students Get Referred for Evaluation for Special Education?

At times, with the rules and regulations that act to protect children from misidentification, administrators may wonder how children ever do end up in special education classes. One typical misnomer in general and special education is that students somehow are *"referred* for special education." In fact, they are referred for further evaluation to determine whether they are eligible for special education services. Students are referred for evaluation in a number of ways:

- The teacher assistance team has persistently (for at least six months) worked with the teacher and the student's parents, and ways to mediate the instructional question or behavioral issue have not been found.
- The student scored lower than the district's predetermined cutoff score on a screening instrument.
- The student scored lower than the predetermined cutoff on a screening instrument administered as part of a community screening activity.
- The student was identified as having special needs by another agency or physician.
- Parents are concerned about the student's eligibility for special education services.

For any of these types of referral, administrators must be aware of cultural and ethnic diversity.

The usual process, beginning with that initial phone call or note regarding referral for further evaluation, is relatively complex. It serves to safeguard both the students' rights concerning confidentiality and misidentification as well as the school's rights in terms of having their programs filled with children who may not be achieving as others wish they would but who are not legally eligible. The process usually includes the following:

(1) A "referral form" is completed. Appended to this form is a description of all other strategies used with the student, the activities of the teacher assistance team regarding the case, and parent and outside agency contacts.

(2) This "referral form" then goes to the school's referral team, who determines whether the form should be sent through to the building administrator. This team may develop "one more thing to try" or members may make observations or find other ways to seek information that may make their decision to proceed or not proceed more accurate.

(3) Parents are called in for a conference. A representative from the school's referral team, the student's teacher, the building administrator, and a professional from the special education program typically will attend. At this meeting, the issues and attempted strategies are discussed; the parents' rights are reviewed with them; and parents are asked to sign a consent form to proceed with the referral, if appropriate.

(4) The evaluation begins. (Guidelines regarding the evaluation process were described earlier in this chapter.)

After the evaluation takes place, the team of professionals who studied the child as well as the parents and the teachers and administrators involved meet to determine whether the child is eligible for special education services. This eligibility is determined by comparing the information gathered about the child with state definitions and criteria. If a child is determined to be eligible, the team proceeds, either at the same or a new meeting, to write an IEP for the child.

The first step in writing the IEP is to describe the child's current level of functioning. This information comes from the evaluation team's and teachers' data. Annual goals and short-term objectives (which the team should be able to complete in three to five months) are developed to address the child's individual needs. The criteria for completion of these goals and objectives are developed. The services needed to meet these goals and objectives are then described and the duration of services indicated. Only after these steps are completed is placement discussed. Placement, as indicated earlier, must both meet the child's individual needs and be in the least restrictive educational alternative. Placement in special education cannot take place without the completion of an IEP.

Key Terms

❑ *Consent.* The parent has been informed of all information relevant to the activity for which consent is sought, agrees in writing, and understands that consent may be revoked at any time (as defined by Public Law 94-142).

❑ *FERPA: Family Educational Rights and Privacy Act (the Buckley Amendment).* A federal statute relating to confidentiality and access to educational records.

❑ *IEP.* Individualized Educational Program.

❑ *Least restrictive environment (LRE).* Using a placement that integrates students with and without disabilities to the greatest extent appropriate.

❑ *Notice.* Information given to parents regarding proposed action to be taken toward their child as well as information about their legal rights.

❑ *Parent.* A parent, guardian, person acting as a parent of a child, or surrogate parent.

❑ *PL 94-142.* The Education for All Handicapped Children Act, now referred to as IDEA (Individuals with Disabilities Education Act).

❑ *Section 504.* The section of the Rehabilitation Act of 1973 providing that recipients of federal assistance may not discriminate on the basis on handicap.

❑ *Special education.* Specially designed instruction, at no cost to the parent, to meet the unique needs of a child with a disability.

Reference

Federal Register. (1977). [Public Law 94-142 regulations, Secs. 300.1-300.589].

NOTES

2

Thorny Issues:
Guidance From the Courts

In addition to federal mandates, case law has generated many requirements regarding students in special education. These issues are far less cut and dried and deal with complex questions. The courts have provided guidance in many areas, including suspension/expulsion, discipline, support and related services, and competency testing.

2.1 Can Special Education Students Be Expelled or Suspended?

Students identified as handicapped must, according to Public Law 94-142, be provided with educational services. They may be expelled or excluded from school, however, if the behavior for which they are being excluded is not a result of the handicapping condition and if federally mandated due process procedures are followed. Expelling a student is considered a change in placement, so all of the procedural guidelines related to Individualized Educational Programs continue to be in place.

In *Goss v. Lopez* (1975), the Supreme Court explained that the 14th Amendment prohibits state officials, including school administrators, from denying students "liberty" or "property" without due process. In this case, hearing and notice were required to precede the removal of a student from school.

Though there is nothing in federal law or regulations concerning the discipline of children in special education that would prohibit short-term suspensions, the Supreme Court in *Honig v. Doe* (1988) ruled that an exclusion from school for more than 10 days is equivalent to a change in placement that cannot be accomplished even because of dangerous behavior. Until proper due process procedures are in place, the child must remain in his or her current placement. The "stay put" provision, the Court ruled, was meant to strip schools of the authority to exclude students with disabilities, particularly those with behavioral disorders, from school. In this case, by refusing to give schools a "dangerousness exception," the Supreme Court indicated that schools must follow the procedures outlined in PL 94-142 and applicable state regulations, beginning with a meeting of the IEP team.

Problem 1. Joseph, an 11th grader in a special education program for students with behavioral disorders, tipped the chair of another student, initiating a classroom brawl. Can Joseph be suspended for five days?

Solution 1. No: As a student with behavioral disorders, it should be anticipated that Joseph would demonstrate socially inappropriate and/or aggressive behaviors. The misbehavior is, within reasonable doubt, related to the handicapping condition.

Problem 2. Marianne, who receives special education services for her visual impairment, is found smoking cigarettes in the rest room. In that this is her third offense, can she be suspended for three days?

Solution 2. It would be difficult to demonstrate that Marianne's cigarette smoking is related to her visual impairment. The student disciplinary code requiring suspension may apply.

2.2 How Can Special Education Students Be Disciplined?

As we mentioned earlier, in the *Honig* case, the Court ruled that the procedures of PL 94-142 must be followed in any suspension or expulsion. But what about other disciplinary measures used in general education?

In *Milonas v. Williams* (1982), the courts held that a school for students with behavioral disorders violated the students' civil rights, as provided by Section 504, by using "behavior modification" methods that included prolonged isolation, physical punishment, and the use of a polygraph, even though parents had given their consent. In addition, any disciplinary measure must follow the "least restrictive environment"; that is, the least intrusive way of dealing with a behavior must be used. The burden of proof, or the duty to substantiate allegations, that less intrusive methods are not appropriate rests on the school administrator.

2.3 How Much Support Must Be Given to Special Education Students?

In *Board of Education v. Rowley* (1985), the Supreme Court rejected previous interpretations of PL 94-142 that the federal law required states to maximize the potential of each handicapped child. Rather, the Supreme Court held that educators must provide sufficient support that the child can benefit from instruction. As long as the procedural requirements are followed and the child is benefiting educationally, the federal law is considered to have been followed. *Adequate educational opportunities* are required; *optimal opportunities* are not.

Problem 3. Sarah, an 11th grader, is making C grades though she is identified as having a learning disability. Her parents argue that, if she had a hired "note-taker," she would be an A student. They request that the resource room teacher arrange for an individual to take notes for Sarah during her lecture classes.

Solution 3. In that Sarah is performing within the average range, this additional support does not need to be provided.

2.4 What Related Services Must Be Provided?

Related services are those necessary for the child to profit from special education. They include such accepted services as transportation and adapted physical education as well as the more controversial medical and psychotherapy services.

A. *Medical Services*

The most common "medical services" question is that of periodic catheterization. A federal court of appeals ruled that, when a service such as catheterization must be performed during school hours by a qualified person, it is a related service. Services that permit a child to remain at school during the day are considered similar to dispensing necessary medicine and administering emergency injections under medical authorization.

B. *Psychotherapy*

The Supreme Court has reasoned that psychotherapy provided by persons who are not physicians would be considered a related service, from the specific authorization of psychological and counseling services. Psychotherapy provided by a physician generally would not be provided. The therapy must be necessary for the child to benefit educationally.

2.5 How Do I Deal With Special Education Students and Competency Tests?

More than half of the states currently require some sort of basic skills test, mostly in math and reading, for high school graduation and promotion or to receive remedial help. Even though it may not seem fair to require special education students to meet competency requirements, high school diplomas can be withheld if

- the test requirement is mandated by the state,
- the way the test is taken is modified so that the test measures achievement and not the handicapping condition (i.e., a test in Braille for a blind student), and
- the student is given a reasonable amount of notice regarding the requirement.

Courts have considered whether minimum competency programs violate PL 94-142 but have found that this law was intended to ensure an appropriate education, and not guarantee an outcome such as a high school diploma. The courts have held that persons who do not meet general requirements are not "otherwise qualified" according to Section 504 of the Rehabilitation Act, so standards do not have to be lowered for students in special education.

Problem 4. Christopher, a student in the fourth grade, receives programming for his specific learning disabilities. His mother argues that the competency test should be read to him, that he will, of course, fail the reading portion of the state-ordered test because he has a reading disability.

Solution 4. In that the achievement test is state ordered and designed to measure reading and not the disability, administering the test in an oral format would be inappropriate.

2.6 Extended Year Programs

In some cases, when a child's educational, social, emotional, or physical development would suffer if education were provided only in the traditional school year, it may be necessary under PL 94-142 and its amendments to make services available for longer periods of time. Lower federal courts have unanimously ruled that policies limiting education to 180 days preclude the consideration of individuals' needs. If included in the IEP, full-year placements, including transportation and other support services, must be provided when needed to avoid regression.

Key Terms

❑ *Related services.* Services necessary for the child to profit from special education.
❑ *"Stay put" provision.* While due process procedures are in place, the child must remain in his or her current placement.

References

Board of Education v. Rowley, 102 S.Ct. (1985).
Goss v. Lopez, 95 S.Ct. 729 (1975).
Honig v. Doe, 108 S.Ct. 592 (1988).
Milonas v. Williams, 491 F.2d 931 (1982).

NOTES

3

Issues Regarding Special Programs

In addition to the traditional special education programs and related services, special considerations emerge when working with students with special needs. These special considerations include those children for whom English is not the primary language, students who are gifted and talented, children with medical issues that may or may not involve special education programming, and the administration of medication.

3.1 Language Issues

In 1974, in a case concerning students of Chinese descent in San Francisco, the Supreme Court indicated that the issue of equality of opportunity was violated when students for whom English was a second language received no instruction to help them learn English. As a result of this suit, it is not enough to provide students for whom English is a second language with the same facilities, books, teachers, and curriculum; specific instruction to meet their needs in learning English must be provided. Unless state law requires a particular approach, schools may choose to offer instruction in English as a second language for several hours each day or week or have separate classrooms for these students with mainstreaming into regular classes when possible. Federal philosophical (but not monetary) support has been ongoing for native-language instruction for students for whom English is a second language.

Problem 1. A family from Guatemala enters your school. Their children are the only Spanish-speaking children in the school. Does instruction in English need to be provided specifically to these two children?

Solution 1. Yes: Instruction in English as a second language must be provided, even if for only a designated number of hours each week.

3.2 Gifted and Talented Children

Federal law does not require that students who are gifted and talented be provided with educational services to meet their unique needs. Not all states therefore have made provisions for these children. Pennsylvania, for example, requires the identification of the gifted and talented in the same way as for other exceptional children. In most states, however, gifted education has not become a high federal or state priority. Students who are gifted and talented need not be provided with alterative or enrichment programs; such activities remain optional.

3.3 Medical Issues That May or May Not Involve Special Education Programming

Two medical issues have been given a great deal of media attention: AIDS and attention deficit disorder.

A. *Children With AIDS*

Children with AIDS may or may not be considered disabled under federal law. Under Public Law 94-142, these children would not be considered disabled unless they require special education and related services. Section 504, however, does provide protection for children with AIDS: Children with AIDS are considered to have an impairment under Section 504 and are therefore protected against discrimination. They are "qualified" to attend school. All school personnel should be especially sensitive to the need for confidentiality and the right to privacy in the cases of children with AIDS.

The Centers for Disease Control (1985) indicate that there have been no identified cases of AIDS infection known to have been transmitted in the school or through other casual person-to-person contact. There are, however, risks to the child with AIDS because there is a greater potential to encounter infection in a school than at home, and children with AIDS are at great risk of suffering severe complications from infections such as chicken pox, herpes simplex, and measles.

The Centers for Disease Control (1985) recommend that decisions regarding the type of educational and care setting for children with AIDS should be based on the behavior, neurological development, and physical condition of the child as well as on the expected type of interaction with others rather than the presence of the disease. They recommend that the benefits of unrestricted school settings outweigh the risks of children acquiring potentially harmful infections in the setting.

B. *Attention Deficit Disorder*

Attention deficit disorder (hyperactivity; ADDH) is a syndrome described in the *Diagnostic and Statistical Manual of the American Psychological Association* (third edition). Children with this disorder are identified as having marked inattention, impulsivity, and hyperactivity, which occurs before the age of 7 and lasts for at least six months. Though recent efforts have been made to include ADD children specifically in the Individuals with Disabilities Education Act, it was felt that most of these children can and should be served in less restrictive environments. Children with ADD may be placed in special education programs if they meet the individual eligibility criteria for those categorical programs. Children with ADD may receive medication, however, to help them manage their behavior.

Problem 2. A parent of a child identified by his psychiatrist as demonstrating ADD has asked that her child be provided special services, including an environmentally different setting (no more than six children in the class, study carrels for each child) and a specially trained teacher. In the multidisciplinary evaluation, data supported that the child demonstrates a learning disability.

Solution 2. An IEP should be written to meet the needs of the child's specific learning disability. The reason for the disability, which may or may not be related to the child's attention deficit disorder, is not relevant in the writing of the IEP. If the parents disagree with the services described in the IEP, due process procedures begin.

3.4 Children on Medication

The most common drug taken to assist children in managing their behavior is methylphenidate, usually known by its brand name Ritalin. Lawsuits have been filed alleging the negligent use of Ritalin with hyperactive children in several states, including suits against school districts for depriving children of due process and for fraud. In one lawsuit, parents and students alleged that the schools, their board members, administrators, physicians, nurses, and the school psychologist pressured them to have the children take Ritalin to control what the schools claimed was hyperactive behavior. The settlement included a lump sum payment and parental notification concerning the dangers attendant on the use of Ritalin, careful medical monitoring, and in-service training of school personnel involved in its use.

More children receive medication to manage attention deficit disorder with hyperactivity than any other childhood disorder: more than 600,000 annually, or between 1% and 2% of the school-age population. Barkley (1990) provides these clinical implications for children with ADD and medication:

- Only 70%-80% respond positively to the medication.
- The use of medication does not lead to enduring changes in the child's behavior.
- There are many side effects that must be monitored, including loss of appetite, sleeplessness, and increases in any tics the child may have.
- Medication should not be the sole treatment used.

Ritalin typically takes effect about 20-30 minutes after the child takes it, and effects last 3 to 4 hours. Ritalin remains the drug of first choice in managing ADDH because of its greater documentation in research, proven efficiency, and greater dose-response information. Other drugs that are used for ADD include Dexedrine (d-amphetamine) and Cylert (pemoline), which are more potent. There are several guidelines for the use of medication to manage ADD:

- The dose should be the lowest possible and should be given only as many times per day as necessary to achieve adequate management of the child's behavior.

- Medication should be discontinued on holidays or summer vacations, unless absolutely necessary.
- The decision to use medication should be based on objective assessment.
- Time should be allowed for evaluation of the effects of the medication.
- Parents should never be given permission to adjust the dosage of medication without prior consultation with the physician.

Another reason students may be taking medication is seizure disorders. Typical medications include phenobarbital, dilantin, tegretol, or zarontin, all of which have the similar possible side effects of drowsiness, loss of balance, dizziness, headaches, nausea, fatigue, and inability to concentrate.

Key Terms

❑ *Attention deficit disorder (hyperactivity).* A diagnostic category described in the *Diagnostic and Statistical Manual of the American Psychological Association* (third edition).

❑ *Ritalin.* A brand name for methylphenidate, a stimulant used to treat attention deficit disorder.

References

American Psychological Association. (1980). *The diagnostic and statistical manual of the American Psychological Association* (3rd ed.). Washington, DC: Author.

Barkley, R. A. (1990). *Attention deficit hyperactivity disorder: A handbook for diagnosis and treatment.* New York: Guilford.

Centers for Disease Control. (1985). Education and foster care of children infected with hymen t-lymphotropic virus type III/lymphadenopathy-associated virus. *Morbidity and Mortality Weekly Report, 34,* 517.

4

Creating Opportunities for Students to Succeed in the Regular Classroom

In this chapter, we describe ways teachers can create opportunities for students with diverse needs to succeed in the regular classroom. These strategies include ways of presenting information that will help support and accommodate students with learning and behavior problems. Such alternatives should be tried before a referral to special education is made to determine whether minor adjustments can address student needs. These strategies are also effective when trying to mainstream a student with an identified disability back into the regular classroom. The primary variable is the teacher; those teachers who are flexible and able to adjust to individual differences are more likely to accommodate the needs of a wide variety of students.

These strategies have been grouped according to common questions teachers have when they try to design instruction to incorporate students with diverse instruction needs. In Chapter 6, problems and alternative strategies across a wide variety of age ranges are offered.

4.1 What Is the Most Important Concern in Developing Opportunities for Students to Be Successful?

A. *Creating a Healthy Environment*

Without a doubt, an environment in which students and adults are respected and needs of students are met is the foundation for providing for the diverse needs of all students. Students experiencing learning and behavior problems are particularly influenced by the deleterious effects of an unhealthy environment. The following are the key components of a healthy environment (Cook, Tessier, & Armbruster, 1987).

(1) Consistency. Very few things unbalance students more than not knowing what is expected and the outcomes for compliance or noncompliance with expectations. When students do not know what to expect, they orient themselves in a defensive posture to fight or flee. As a result, both teachers and students become edgy and deviances within the environment become greatly accentuated.

(2) Smooth transitions. Transitions are valuable times in every classroom. When students don't know when or how to change from one activity or environment, chaos often results

and the teacher can lose control. Misbehavior is likely to result and valuable instructional time will be lost trying to regain order.

(3) Limits. Reasonable public limits or rules must be established. Although students must have the freedom to express themselves and be autonomous, they often lack judgment and need guidelines to establish appropriate behavior. The need for limits is particularly relevant in elementary and preschool students, and limits help them develop an appropriate sense of self-control. It is critical, however, that teachers strike a delicate balance between limits and fulfilling the need for freedom of expression. The following guidelines may help the teacher establish this balance:

1. Only limits that are absolutely critical to a positive learning environment should be established.
2. Limits should focus on what is expected in positive terms rather than being stated in negative terms. For example, "students and adults treat each other with respect" rather than "no name calling."
3. Limits must be reasonable and consistent with the developmental level of students. For example, having preschool and kindergarten students sit in their seats for long periods of time is unreasonable.
4. Consequences to limits must be enforceable. Establishing a consequence for a limit that is not enforceable invites a challenge and brings the credibility of the teacher into question. The most effective consequences for compliance or noncompliance with rules are those that naturally occur.

(4) Open expression of ideas and feelings. An environment in which feelings and ideas can be freely but appropriately expressed diffuses conflict and demonstrates respect.

4.2 What Teaching Strategies Can Help Students With Mild Learning Problems Participate?

A. *Taping*

Students who have difficulty with reading but have the cognitive ability to be in classes with their age-mates can benefit from taped recordings of presentations and tests. Taping readings and lectures also allows students to go back and review information, which further enhances understanding. Use of volunteers and other students can be an efficient way to make recordings. Furthermore, this strategy can help provide students with a sense of responsibility and confidence.

B. *Pacing*

One of the most important aspects of a lesson is the rate at which the lesson progresses (Kindsvatter, Wilen, & Ishler, 1988). A quick pace maintains student attention and is appropriate when students have attention problems. Some students have difficulty with quick responses, however, and can be intimidated by a pace that is too fast. In this case, the teacher should show patience and allow adequate time for these students to reflect and respond.

C. *Prompts*

The primary reason for providing prompts is to gain student attention either visually or auditorially. For example, visual prompts could be a look from the teacher, an object, or a symbol (such as stickers, circles, check marks). Such items could be placed on the desk or paper as a reminder to stay on task, in his or her seat, or whatever goal is appropriate for that student. Auditory prompts can also be effective, such as "this is important" or "listen carefully." Another option of auditory cuing could be a bell or timer to signal when work should be complete. Whatever approach is chosen, the principal objective should be to provide a reminder to the teacher and/or student regarding the task at hand. Such prompts should be selected according to the needs of the child and should not call undue attention to the child.

D. *Breaking Tasks Into Smaller Steps*

Dividing assignments into segments of shorter tasks helps facilitate students' ability to complete tasks and be successful. An effective modification of this approach is to allow the pupils to set their own goals. It is important to remember, however, that these goals should be realistic for the learner, because pupils are often unrealistic and can pick too large or too small a section to complete.

E. *Corrective Feedback*

Providing students with feedback on their performance is an important way to reinforce concepts and to guide students to correct performance. Listed below are guidelines for providing good corrective feedback:

1. Provide feedback often and as soon as possible after the action.
2. Dignify student's incorrect responses and provide prompts to help the student move to a more appropriate response. For example, "Abe Lincoln was a good try, but I had a more recent president in mind."
3. Make feedback specific and focus on the positive. Feedback should encourage rather than discourage the student.
4. Keep feedback at the correct developmental level. Feedback that is too detailed and beyond the grasp of students will only add to their confusion.

F. Reduce Concepts

Helping teachers to reduce the number of concepts introduced at any one time is an important technique to help students with mild learning and behavior problems stay in the regular classroom. It is important that the teacher make sure one idea is understood before moving on to another topic. Students tend not to feel overwhelmed by the total assignment and also immediately feel as if they are accomplishing their work. For example, you could suggest that the teacher cut questions, math problems, and so on into strips and give the student one strip to finish at one time. You also might suggest that the teacher assign a smaller portion of the lesson and tell students that, if they achieve a certain success rate, such as 80%, the remaining portion of the lesson could be omitted or assigned for extra credit.

What are some other ways that teachers can support students having difficulty so that they can participate in a lesson?

Plan Practice Sessions

Targeting times during the day or week for drill and practice for those students who are having trouble can be a powerful way to avoid problems. An ideal way to manage this procedure is to use tutors or aides. Practice and drill sessions are especially useful for developing a foundation of basic skills (e.g., production of letter forms in handwriting; service work in reading, multiplication tables, and proper language forms). With support and guidance, a teacher can easily develop a "catch-up" period to be incorporated into the calendar (e.g., every Friday from 11:30 to 12:00). At this time, students can do additional drill and practice or catch up on assignments, take makeup tests or retest, enjoy enrichment activities, have free time, or receive specific individual support.

Tutoring

Tutoring is a system of accepting assistance within the classroom from other children or from people other than the teacher, such as parents, paraprofessionals, students, or volunteers. Tutoring in this context occurs when more than one student is accepting help at the same time with a specific subject or practice. Such practices are an interesting way to get the community involved in your school. Perhaps a business could adopt your school and provide release time for employees to be tutors.

Using other students as tutors has advantages over using volunteers and aides or paraprofessionals for two specific reasons: (a) Student tutors are more readily available than additional personnel, often due to a lack of funding or personnel shortages, and (b) when tutors and students switch roles, both benefit. Students working with other students can help the overworked teacher and frustrated student and provide an opportunity for other students to grow and have a feeling of accomplishment. When older students tutor younger students, it is called "cross-age tutoring." Frequently, this is a solution for teachers who think their own students are not ready for tutoring each other but want individualized instruction in their classrooms.

To help teachers in your school develop an effective tutoring system, the following steps should be stressed:

1. Provide training sessions for tutors. Don't assume children will know how to teach other children.
2. Set aside preparation time for tutors to work with others in preparing tutoring materials so that the time spent in a tutorial session can be of maximum benefit (Cloward, 1967; Frager & Stern, 1970; Heron & Harris, 1987; Johnson & Bailey, 1974).
3. Make special arrangements for the missed class time of the tutors. Sometimes credit can be given to students participating as tutors.
4. Monitor tutors as they work with their assigned students.

Cooperative Learning

This is a powerful strategy to accommodate the needs of a wide variety of students learning the same lesson. Students of mixed abilities are purposely grouped together and encouraged to work collaboratively to support each other in accomplishing common group goals. The reward system is based on the overall performance of the group rather than on individual performance. There are many forms and variations on cooperative learning structures (see Arends, 1991), but Slavin (1983) has identified several features common to these approaches:

1. Students collaborate in teams to master academic materials.
2. Teams are made up of students with a wide range of abilities.
3. The reward structure is based on the performance of the group rather than the individual performance of group members.

4.3 What Are Some Ways to Help Students Get Ready for a Lesson or Activity?

A. *Modeling*

Demonstrating the skill or activity to be learned often is a very effective technique. One of the most important factors for students in retaining information is active versus passive involvement in the lesson. With younger children, the teacher might actually guide the student through the activity. For example, the teacher might take the student's hand and actually move him or her through the motions of making the letter P. With older students, role-playing situations can be effective, particularly if teachers can use role-playing to help these students understand appropriate behavior in social situations.

Studies have shown that role-playing was more effective than lectures and discussion with high school students.

B. *Preteach Vocabulary*

A simple way to aid students with mild learning disabilities is to preteach key words in a lesson. Flash cards can be made by the teacher, an aide, volunteer, or other students. One of these individuals can then spend two or three minutes during several days going over words. Once cards are made, they can be used for future lessons. Sometimes highlighting words in text and spending time with the student and/or working with parents in going over words prior to the lesson can be an effective technique.

4.4 What Are Some Strategies to Ensure Students Understand the Assignment They Have Been Given?

A. *Introducing Topics*

An important concept for teachers to understand is that, when introducing various tasks and considering the requirements of those tasks, entry to and closure of the lesson are of the utmost importance to the student's success (Shostock, 1982). Entry into a lesson is the pupil's first contact with the content of the lesson. It is important to think about focusing the class's attention in interesting and atypical ways. Kindsvatter et al. (1988) provide examples of ways entry could be used in introducing tasks within the classroom:

1. Use personal comments or casual conversational remarks to increase student attention. In fact, doing something un-

expected or sensational as an introduction to new information can focus students' attention on the task at hand.

2. Be sure students understand the relevance of the content to other areas. Providing an advanced organizer, such as a summary of what will be learned in an upcoming lesson, can be an effective entry technique.

B. *Providing Closure*

As was previously discussed, the close of a lesson is important to the understanding of the lesson and serves as a bridge to the next lesson or activity. The following are strategies you could use to help teachers provide good closure:

1. Summarize the content in concise bullet lists.
2. Show students how to integrate the concepts they were taught with what they have previously learned.
3. Help students to see how and when to apply concepts they have learned.
4. Point out accomplishments of students in reaching stated goals of the lesson to motivate students and to reinforce their accomplishments.
5. Preview an upcoming activity or lesson to provide a bridge and help ensure a smooth transition.

C. *Clarifying Directions*

It is surprising how encouraging teachers to take the time to ensure that all students understand and are clear on how to complete an assignment can avoid a whole range of problems. Often students have problems or act out because they don't understand what is to be done and not because they have some internal learning problem. Both oral and written directions should be integrated whenever possible in attempting to assure the student is clear on the task. Bickart et al. (1988) provide brief pointers on how to clarify both written and oral directions:

Oral Directions

1. Use simple language and don't speak too quickly.
2. Repeat key points for emphasis.
3. Make sure students are attending as you talk.
4. Provide only one or two directions at a time to avoid confusion.
5. Post a written copy of standard classroom rules.
6. Write complex or multiple directions on the board or on an overhead or hand them out when necessary.
7. Request students to repeat the directions immediately after they are given, to check accuracy and increase comprehension.
8. Tell the students to, or help them to, write down the directions.
9. Reinforce students for following directions.
10. Tape-record directions so that the child can repeat them as many times as needed.

Written Directions

1. Make sure the directions are clearly written.
2. Use simple and concise language.
3. Number each step.
4. Provide examples when possible.
5. Have the students that you suspect will have confusion explain the directions to you before beginning the assignment.
6. Reinforce students for following directions.
7. Highlight or underline important concepts in cooperative learning—a teaching strategy in which students work in mixed ability groups and are rewarded for group performance rather than individual performance.

Key Terms

❑ *Corrective feedback.* Information given to students regarding their performance.

❑ *Limits.* Public rules regulating behavior.

❑ *Modeling.* Providing a demonstration of the skill or activity.

❑ *Pacing.* The tempo of the lesson.

❑ *Prompt.* A means to gain student attention.

❑ *Tutoring.* A system of accepting assistance within the classroom from other children or teachers, that is, persons other than teachers.

References

Arends, R. (1991). *Learning to teach.* Columbus, OH: Charles E. Merrill.

Bickart, K., Donahue, G., Gomik, M., Grassi, P., Peters, H., & Rowan, M. (1988). *How to live til Friday.* Cleveland, OH: Friday.

Cloward, R. D. (1967). Studies in tutoring. *Journal of Experimental Education, 36,* 14-25.

Cook, R., Tessier, A., & Armbruster, V. (1987). *Adapting early childhood curricula for children with special needs.* Columbus, OH: Charles E. Merrill.

Frager, S., & Stern, C. (1970). Learning by teaching. *The Reading Teacher, 23,* 403-417.

Heron, T. E., & Harris, K. C. (1987). *The educational consultant.* Austin, TX: Pro-ed.

Johnson, M., & Bailey, J. S. (1974). Cross-age tutoring: Fifth grade as arithmetic tutors for kindergarten children. *Journal of Applied Behavioral Analysis, 7,* 223-235.

Kindsvatter, R., Wilen, W., & Ishler, M. (1988). *Dynamics of effective teaching.* White Plains, NY: Longman.

Shostock, R. (1982). *Lesson presenting skill: Classroom teaching[?] skills.* Lexington, MA: D. C. Heath.

Slavin, R. (1983). *Cooperative learning.* White Plains, NY: Longman.

5

Helping Students Change Inappropriate Behavior

The previous chapter discussed strategies to create a positive learning environment that supports children with special needs within the regular classroom and provides them with opportunities to succeed. Sometimes students display behaviors that draw negative attention to themselves and that greatly inhibit their ability to be successful in the regular classroom. Often creating a supportive learning environment is all that is needed to change these behaviors. Other times, however, teachers need to work on changing particular aspects of students' behavior so that students can more readily benefit from learning opportunities. In this chapter, we present ways to change behavior and, in Chapter 6, we demonstrate how these strategies can be applied in real situations.

5.1 What Are Common Ways to Change Student Behavior in Routine Teaching Practice?

A. *Reprimands*

A reprimand is a form of feedback used by teachers to stop inappropriate behavior, which needs careful self-monitoring so that it is not overused or inappropriately used. Quiet reprimands are always more effective than loud reprimands. Providing quiet reprimands in close proximity while making eye contact is most effective. Finally, the less reprimands are used, the better. Something is obviously wrong if a reprimand is given again and again. Students are more likely to respond in a positive way when they are treated in a positive way.

B. *Effective Praise*

All students need to be praised and encouraged. It is impossible for teachers to provide too much praise and encouragement. Praise can, however, be detrimental if it is not handled correctly. Brophy and Good (1986), Kindsvatter, Wilen, and Ishler (1988), and others have cautioned teachers to carefully analyze the praising of behaviors that reflect the teacher's own thinking and needs rather than those behaviors reflecting student learning style and needs. It is critical for teachers to understand that focusing on their own needs limits student development by tending to conform the students to becoming like the teacher and not be themselves. Praise must be honest and individualized to respond to each student uniquely. Some important steps to providing effective praise and encouragement follow:

(1) Make sure the praise given is specific. Phrases like "that's a very neat paper" or "thanks for helping me straighten the room" are far more effective than "good boy" or "you're wonderful" or "good job."

(2) Recognize the power of nonverbal praise and encouragement and use a look, a wink, a pat on the back, and so on to encourage. Nonverbal gestures are more subtle and can be very effective with older students.

(3) Be sure to vary the words and phrases you use to encourage students. Using the same words or phrases over and over again will cause them to lose their power.

(4) It is important that praise be used when it is deserved. Giving phoney praise is easily seen through by students and can call into question the credibility of other applications of praise.

c. *Ignoring Behavior*

The opposite of praising is ignoring behaviors. Not attending to a behavior is a powerful way to extinguish a behavior, but it isn't always the best technique. When misbehavior is an effort on the part of the student to gain teacher attention, ignoring is effective. When this is not the intent of the student, ignoring will not be effective and might serve to escalate the behavior. Several other points to remember when considering ignoring as a strategy are described below.

(1) First the teacher should determine that the student's behavior is an effort to gain attention. There are no pat or easy ways to tell. Sometimes a teacher can tell through subtle signs from the student. Dreikurs, Grumwald, and Pepper (1971) have suggested that a teacher's reaction to the behavior is an indicator of the intent of the behavior. If a teacher is feeling annoyed, often a student is seeking that teacher's attention.

(2) Often when ignoring a behavior, the behavior will increase. This is called the spike effect and is the student's attempt to increase disruption to gain that teacher's attention. You need to stress to teachers the need to be persistent.

(3) Frequently, it will help if others know that the disruptive behavior is an effort to get attention. When teachers and adults are provided with this information, they can ignore the behavior as well and help to change the behavior.

(4) Pairing ignoring with praising is an essential component to change the student's behavior. Other students also can help ignore behaviors. Praising students for appropriate behavior while ignoring disruptive behavior is a very powerful approach. Without it, the method of ignoring will not work.

5.2 Are There Special Programs or Strategies Teachers Can Apply?

A. *Public Posting*

The underlying reason for public posting is to provide students with a visual reminder of their progress. There are a variety of ways to publicly post student progress; examples include recording students' daily quiz scores or posting the percentage of change in disruptive hall behavior on a large poster board. If some students have much lower scores than the whole class, this technique should not be chosen because it can cause further differences. Recording group progress and making rewards contingent upon a minimum level, however, can be a way to engender cooperation among students to aid those with mild learning and behavior problems. To enhance the power of public posting, it is important that teachers combine verbal feedback, praise, and encouragement with the visual feedback.

B. *Contingency Contracting*

This is a method that can be used to individualize instruction and modify inappropriate behavior by responding to the student's interest, needs, and abilities. Contingency contracting can be applied to the cognitive, affective, and psychomotor domains of learning (Walker & Shea, 1986) and involves a written explanation of contingencies to be used by a student's teacher or parent (Homme, Csanyi, Gonzales, & Rechs, 1970). In simple terms, the contract is actually an agreement that delineates specific behaviors that the student will implement and the consequences that will result. Such contracts mirror what happens in our society. Contracting is a positive and simple way to incorporate student interests, needs, and abilities into a systematic behavior change plan. It is a powerful technique that encourages the student to become an active participant in improving his or her own behavior. Contingency contracts can be designed to be implemented at home or at school. Home-based contracts are delivered in the home and require a strong working arrangement between parents and teachers. Both types of contracts are binding and can be simple or complex depending on the age of the student. The following are some guidelines to use when developing a contract:

1. Develop all aspects of the contract with all parties involved. This will help ensure that the rewards are meaningful to the student.
2. Be sure that the contract is written in terms that are easily understood by the student.
3. Make sure that the terms of the contract are stated in a positive way.
4. Target a specific behavior to work on and clearly define everyone's responsibilities. Be sure each contract includes the following information:
   the student's responsibilities,
   the consequence for fulfilling the student's responsibilities,

who will provide the consequence,
when the consequence will occur, and
how long the consequence will last and how long the contract will be in force.

5. Provide encouragement for progress toward fulfilling the contract.

6. Keep accurate records of performance so that the student can see his or her progress.

7. Review the contract and allow opportunity for renegotiating if the contract isn't working.

8. Develop a plan to phase out contracts when new patterns of behavior have been established.

c. Token Economies

This is a system in which tokens are awarded for the desired behavior. Such a system may work when praise and attention have not worked. Tokens can be any number of things: points, check marks, stars, chips, stamps, stickers, play money, happy faces, and so on. The tokens in the system function as money does in our society. Guidelines for using a token economy are as follows:

1. It is important that the behaviors that will result in the provision of tokens are clearly defined. The target behaviors should be posted for everyone to view easily. Students also need to know when and where they can exchange their tokens and who monitors the exchange.

2. The tokens selected should be durable, easily available, and easy to administer. Using checks or stars on a poster or record card can prevent counterfeit or theft.

3. To determine appropriate reinforcers, students should be involved in the selection of reinforcers.

4. A balance should be struck so that the students do not earn reinforcers too quickly but are not required to work too hard for reinforcers.
5. Develop a plan to phase out the token economy when the desired behaviors are a part of the students' repertoire. Some suggestions follow:

    Increase the time between opportunities for exchanging tokens for reinforcers.

    Make the schedule for receiving tokens more intermittent, or decrease the number of behaviors that will earn a token.

D. *Spell-a-Word Game*

An interesting strategy that is particularly successful with younger children is the spell-a-word game. First, the student and the teacher choose a reinforcer such as a sticker, free time, the chance to take messages to the principal, or the like. The student then works for letters to spell out the reinforcer.

E. *Report Card Home*

Providing a weekly or daily report card home can be a positive method of reinforcing a child's efforts. It is also a way to keep parents informed and have parents become active participants by having them offer reinforcement for achievements made at school. Parents should understand the importance of their role and should also realize that reinforcers do not have to be expensive and can be special treats or attention. Also, it is critical that teachers focus the plan so that it is positive. It would be inappropriate for this to become a vehicle for always informing the parents about things the student isn't doing.

5.3 Are There Ways to Use Peers to Help Change Students' Inappropriate Behavior?

A. *Group Goal Setting*

Students are placed into groups and then set goals for themselves. Students meet on a structured schedule and provide feedback to each other on their progress. The goals must be specific and the teacher should help students break larger goals into small attainable target behaviors when needed. With some minimal structure, middle and high school students are well able to lead their own groups. A teacher should be the facilitator for student groups.

B. *Timer Game*

In this game, a group contingency for appropriate behavior is specified for a specific time period. All members receive the reward if the contingency is met. The length of time will vary according to the age of the student, and initially time intervals should be short.

C. *Peer Monitoring*

This is a system in which peers are trained to issue and withdraw points from their classmates. This is a variation of the token economy in that tokens are exchanged for previously decided upon reinforcers. The parameters of this system must be taught to the students before it can be implemented. First, the teacher should model the system by running it for several days. These days essentially may be viewed as a training phase and, once the teacher is sure students understand the system, two or more cocaptains are chosen. These students are then responsible for issuing or withdrawing points for the class. Typically, each cocaptain has responsibility for a part of the class, and cocaptains change on a weekly basis.

D. *Good Behavior Game*

A variation on group contingency is the good behavior game. Students are divided into teams and compete to provide appropriate behavior in the classroom. The class is divided into two teams that compete to see who can follow class rules the best. A criterion should be set so that some students can make mistakes. For example, the teacher can establish that 80% of each team's members are required to reach the criterion to receive the reinforcement. If the criterion doesn't allow for some mistakes, students with more serious behavior problems may end up being ridiculed by team members or sabotage the team by acting out.

5.4 What About Using the Student Who Is Experiencing the Problem as a Change Agent?

A. *Self-Monitoring*

Self-monitoring is a process by which students monitor their own progress toward a goal. The first step is to select a target behavior to be changed. Once the target behavior has been identified, the teacher and student should work together to define the behavior in the student's terms. Next, a practical method for the student to measure the behavior is selected. Sometimes just having students monitor their behavior is enough to change the behavior in a desired way. The teacher, however, may choose to set up contingencies for the student to receive a reinforcer for achieving a desired goal.

B. *Self-Evaluation*

An extension of self-monitoring is self-evaluation. This procedure differs from self-monitoring in that it requires the students to assess the quality of behaviors as opposed to simply counting the behaviors. To start a self-evaluation system, the teacher and the student both examine and jointly target behaviors to change and then develop goals for future behavior. They then develop a system to evaluate progress toward goals. For example, the following system might be used to evaluate compliance with classroom rules:

5 = Excellent: All classroom rules were followed during the entire interval; work completed was 90%-100% correct.

4 = Very Good: All classroom rules were followed during the interval; work was 80%-90% correct.

3 = Average: Generally followed rules and any infractions were of a minor nature; work was 70%-80% correct.

2 = Below Average: One or more rules were broken with unacceptable behavior; work completed was 60%-70% correct.

1 = Unacceptable: One or more rules were broken during the interval; engaged in inappropriate behavior most of the time; work completed was 0%-60% accurate.

Initially, the teacher meets with the student on a daily basis to review progress. As time goes on, intervals between meetings can be extended. This approach has been quite successful with helping students with identified disabilities adapt to the regular classroom. It is equally powerful as a way to establish and maintain the appropriate behavior of other students not formally identified as having a disability but experiencing problems within the regular classroom (Rhode, Morgan, & Young, 1983).

C. *Self-Instruction*

This is a procedure in which activities are used step-by-step to cause improvement. When establishing an instruction program, the first step is to analyze the activity to be accomplished by breaking it down into its necessary steps. For example, if the student's target behavior is to begin seat work assignments independently during seat work time, the necessary steps would include task demands, planning statements, self-guiding instruction, coping statements for errors, and self-praise statements. The teacher should develop steps with the student, which should be written in the student's own words. For example, a self-instruction plan for seat work might read: "To do a good job in seat work, I have to get my work folder out by 9 o'clock, read my work plan, and begin working. I have to take my time, stay in my seat, and raise my hand when I need help. I did it! Good for me!" When this plan is first developed, the teacher should walk through the steps with the student, saying the words together. Later, the teacher whispers the instructions while the student says them aloud. Finally, the student should be able to implement the steps alone (Albion, 1980).

Key Terms

- ❏ *Contingency contracting.* Providing a written explanation of expectations and their related consequences.
- ❏ *Good behavior game.* A form of group contingency in which students are broken into teams that compete to see which team can follow the rules best.
- ❏ *Peer monitoring.* A system in which peers are trained to administer or withdraw points to their peers based on their performance.
- ❏ *Public posting.* Listing of names to provide students with visual feedback on their progress.
- ❏ *Reprimands.* Verbal feedback to stop inappropriate behavior.
- ❏ *Token economy.* Tokens are used to reinforce behavior; these tokens then may be used to purchase a reward privilege.

References

Albion, F. M. (1980). *Development and implementation of self-monitoring / self-instruction procedures in the classroom.* Paper presented at the Council for Exceptional Children's 58th Annual International Convention, Philadelphia.

Brophy, J., & Good, T. (1986). *Teacher's behavior and student achievement: Handbook on research and teaching.* New York: Macmillan.

Dreikurs, R., Grumwald, B. B., & Pepper, F. (1971). *Maintaining sanity in the classroom: Illustrated teaching techniques.* New York: Harper & Row.

Homme, L. C., Csanyi, A. P., Gonzales, M. A., & Rechs, J. R. (1970). *How to use contingency contracting in the classroom.* Champaign, IL: Research Press.

Kindsvatter, R., Wilen, W., & Ishler, M. (1988). *Dynamics of effective teaching.* White Plains, NY: Longman.

Rhode, G., Morgan, D., & Young, K. (1983). Generalization and maintenance of treatment gains of behaviorally handicapped students from resource rooms to regular classrooms using self-evaluation procedures. *Journal of Applied Behavior Analysis, 16,* 171-188.

Walker, J. E., & Shea, T. M. (1986). *Behavior management: A practical approach for educators.* Columbus, OH: Charles E. Merrill.

6

Students Who Challenge the System: Examples and Solutions

In the previous two chapters, we suggested strategies that can be used to accommodate the needs of students with learning and behavior problems within the regular classroom. Chapter 4 focused on teaching strategies that can be used to create opportunities for students who challenge the system to succeed in the classroom. In Chapter 5, we presented strategies to modify the inappropriate behavior of students so that they can develop the ability to be more successful in the regular classroom. In this chapter, we describe a variety of real classroom problems across a variety of situations to illustrate the use of these strategies. The type of strategies addressed in Chapter 4 will be called "teaching strategies" and the type of strategies discussed in Chapter 5 will be called "behavior change strategies."

6.1 Challenge: Grade 1

Your art class is making "holiday theme collages," which require coloring, pasting, and drawing. Contessa, a first grader, is having difficulty manipulating the scissors, pasting neatly, and drawing a recognizable picture. Increasingly frustrated as the project wears on, Contessa begins roaming around the room disturbing others by talking loudly and asking, "Is it time to go yet?" What can you do?

A. *Teaching Strategies*

(1) Requiring Contessa to complete tasks of this nature may be expecting too much from her given her undeveloped fine motor skills. Breaking the task down into smaller segments may be helpful. For instance, completing an art activity only requiring that she use scissors would be appropriate, particularly if the task involved cutting along a dotted straight line printed in large type. As her fine motor skills improve, Contessa could cut more complex designs.

(2) Divide the assignment into less complex segments. For instance, one day could be spent cutting pictures, the next day, pasting, and the next, drawing. In this situation, the nature of the art activity may be too complex, and the chances for success may be enhanced by breaking the skills down into more manageable units.

(3) Whenever tasks require that Contessa use fine motor skills, it is important that each skill be modeled for her. For example, show Contessa the proper way to use paste or scissors.

(4) Drawing is a questionable activity for Contessa at the current time. Art activities should focus on helping her to improve her fine motor skills. For example, have Contessa trace pictures along dotted lines and practice coloring between the lines.

(5) Art activities that do not require as much fine motor coordination are more appropriate for Contessa. Activities such as finger painting or brush painting on large paper require less coordination and also would increase the likelihood of success for Contessa.

(6) Allow Contessa to complete an alternative assignment that does not require a great deal of fine motor coordination. For example, the above assignment could be adapted for Contessa by allowing her to make hand impressions using watercolors to form a Christmas tree pattern.

(7) During drawing tasks, allow Contessa to use form boards or tracing patterns to improve her fine motor skills. For example, using farm animal stencils to make a scenic picture would allow Contessa to practice her fine motor skills and at the same time help her to complete a project. Gradually fade these materials as her skills improve.

(8) Use different mediums to allow Contessa to artistically express her creativity. For example, let her splash paint and make interesting designs. Or you might allow her to use clay to make abstract figures.

B. *Behavior Management Techniques*

(1) Reward Contessa for improved approximations rather than for perfect performance. For example, if Contessa is given a series of straight lines to cut, reward her for each improved performance. Effective rewards for this age group include stickers, stars, and teacher praise. Reward her for each improved performance rather than for perfect performance.

(2) By carefully reducing the demands of the task (as described above), Contessa's acting-out behavior may naturally fade. If not, when she is given a frustrating task, don't let her behavior escalate to the point of acting out. Be sensitive to her needs. For example, when you sense her beginning to experience failure, change the assignment to something at which she can feel successful (e.g., finger painting). Once she's made the change and her behavior remains appropriate, reward her for appropriate behavior.

(3) Although the above modification requires that the teacher intervene before the acting-out behavior occurs, there may be an occasion when the teacher wants to teach Contessa task perseverance (e.g., when the teacher wants to increase the level of difficulty of the designs to be cut). In this case, make sure that the complexity of the designs is gradually introduced and that Contessa is not overwhelmed by designs given to her that are too difficult. Task analyze the skill of cutting designs. To conduct a task analysis, arrange the skill of cutting designs from least complex to most complex. For example, have Contessa cut straight lines first, then simple angles, then rectangles or squares, then circles or wavy lines, and so on. Whenever Contessa becomes frustrated, drop down to a less complex skill. Reward her efforts and provide rewards for appropriate behavior as the skills become increasingly complex.

6.2 Challenge: Grade 3

Suzy constantly wants your attention. She asks unnecessary questions, interrupts others when they are speaking to you, and says you don't like her when you give attention to other students. She belittles others when you praise them and then comments, "You never say that to me." What can you do?

A. *Teaching Strategies*

(1) Suzy's excessive need for attention most likely stems from poor self-esteem. She wants your praise to boost her self-esteem. Therefore handle this behavior delicately and with sensitivity. A good approach might be to set a specific time aside each day as a special time for you and Suzy. Let her know when she starts to demand your attention that she has this specific time to talk to you. Then ask her to wait. Make sure you follow through.

(2) Make sure that Suzy understands that her behavior is hurtful to the other students. Take Suzy aside and explain to her that others need your attention as well.

(3) Arrange to incorporate activities designed to improve self-esteem. For example, have Suzy complete an "I Can" book that lists all the things she does well. As Suzy attains new skill levels in your class, have her add them to this book. This activity will help Suzy to focus on her own accomplishments, boosting her self-esteem.

(4) A good strategy is to greet Suzy when you come in each morning with a special smile. Ask her how she's doing and spend a little bit of time engaging in small talk.

(5) Make sure that Suzy's tasks are appropriate for her ability and that they ensure success. Make special efforts to let Suzy know when you think she's done well and has made unusual efforts. Given her poor self-esteem, plan activities that will help her to feel she's making progress and is a capable person.

(6) Give Suzy feedback regarding her work as soon as possible. This will help her feel more secure. Grade her papers promptly and make efforts to give her feedback regarding her mistakes that is not negative. For instance, if Suzy makes regrouping errors on a subtraction worksheet, show her where her errors are in the process of regrouping and allow her to correct her answers before assigning a grade.

B. *Behavior Management Techniques*

(1) Ignore Suzy's attention-getting behaviors and reward her with your attention when she is behaving appropriately and not seeking your attention. By doing this, you will be teaching Suzy that your attention is contingent upon her appropriate behavior.

(2) Make sure that, when you do have to reprimand Suzy, you let her know that it is her behavior you dislike, not her. For example, you might say, "Suzy, when you interrupt while I'm talking with someone else, I feel angry. When you wait your turn, however, I am happy to speak to you." This statement lets Suzy know the specific reaction you have to her interrupting and also suggests a behavior that she can choose the next time.

(3) Contract with Suzy to spend special time with you for good behavior. For example, you might use a check or point system and incorporate the following objectives to be checked at specific periods of time:

(a) waits turn
(b) asks for teacher attention appropriately
(c) makes positive comments about self

Using the combination of the contract and check system, you and Suzy can determine a minimal criterion of checks or points she has to receive each day to spend time with you.

(4) Whenever you see Suzy behaving appropriately, present her with a "Positive Person Paper." The idea behind this technique is to surprise Suzy and reward her for appropriate behavior. You can post the paper in the class or allow her to take it home to show her parents. If Suzy has done something especially positive, you can provide her with a reward such as free time or computer time—whatever is rewarding to her. She'll enjoy the special attention, and her behavior will improve dramatically if you use this procedure consistently.

6.3 Challenge: Grade 4

Your class is working on a math worksheet. It contains several rows of problems. Robbie seems to be overwhelmed by the entire page of problems and has difficulty focusing on one row at a time. He gives up on math and takes out his coloring book and begins to color. What can you do?

A. *Teaching Strategies*

(1) If worksheets are too frequently used in your class and are used as a means of drill, change the manner in which you present the task. For example, have children complete computational or math comprehension problems by placing the problems on a small deck of cards. Make an answer key. Have students use a generic game board. Before moving on spaces, they must correctly answer the problem on the card. Allow them to check their answers on the key. Use of this activity would be particularly appropriate for Robbie as he would need to focus only on one problem at a time.

(2) Place only a few of the problems on the page in large print and have Robbie complete one page at a time and then turn it in. Then he can proceed to each successive page until he has completed the entire assignment.

(3) Reduce the number of problems Robbie must complete. Although drill is important, for some students, an overwhelming number of problems is defeating. Give Robbie enough problems to cover the content you are teaching to ensure his mastery but limit the overall number in drill exercises.

(4) Cut the worksheet into strips along the rows and have Robbie complete the strips one by one.

B. *Behavior Management Techniques*

Contract with Robbie to complete a minimum number of problems. Then have Robbie complete the specified minimum number of problems and give him points or tokens for completing additional problems. Chart the number of additional problems each day so that he can see his progress.

6.4 Challenge: Grade 6

Although your class has rules for appropriate lunchroom behavior, Tommy continues to be disruptive in the cafeteria. He breaks in ahead of others in line, can't keep his hands off others, throws food, and generally is loud. A good and mostly well-behaved student during class, you are having difficulty understanding why this behavior occurs only in the cafeteria. What can you do?

A. *Teaching Strategies*

(1) Structure the routine of lunch if it is not already an established, well-organized routine. For example, you might systematically rotate the order of the lines by allowing the first person in the first row to be first one day, the second person in the first row to be first the next day, and so forth. That way, it will be clear who is to be first. Also, make clear rules about breaking in line, putting hands on others, and the routine for dismissal (e.g., one table at a time). These kinds of structures may alleviate much of Tommy's inappropriate behavior simply because the rules are clearer to him.

(2) Prepare a miniunit for the class on dining etiquette and have your students develop clear, concise cafeteria rules. This way, you can be sure Tommy knows proper etiquette, and the rules developed by your class will be more enforceable.

B. *Behavior Management Techniques*

(1) Using a goal sheet and point system, contract with Tommy for a minimal criterion of expected performance each day. When this criterion is met, immediately reward Tommy for his good lunchroom behavior.

(2) As Tommy's behavior is an attempt to get attention, and is limited to the cafeteria, it is possible that the unstructured nature of lunch is contributing to Tommy's behavior. Structure lunch as much as possible for him. For example, have an established routine for lining up for lunch. When Tommy breaks ahead in line, make sure that he goes to the end of the line. This way, Tommy will begin to think twice about doing it in the future.

(3) Another way of structuring the lunch period is to assign Tommy to sit alone and away from others when he misbehaves. Make his return contingent upon the completion of a "Consideration Paper." The Consideration Paper requires Tommy to identify and think through his misbehavior, suggest alternatives, and then make amends for his inappropriate behavior. For example, if Tommy threw food in the lunchroom, restrict his seating until he has completed and received your approval on a Consideration Paper. As part of completing the Consideration Paper, Tommy must propose some sort of restitution for his misbehavior. Whatever restitution Tommy proposes, make sure it is directly connected with the inappropriate act. For instance, restitution for throwing food in the cafeteria would be to clean up the food or spend some time helping out in the lunchroom. Having Tommy work through this process will teach him appropriate cafeteria behavior and will allow him to connect the "causes and effects" of his inappropriate behavior.

6.5 Challenge: Grade 9

You are showing a film in your English class. As you begin the film, you notice that Joe is staring out the window. Although you have told the class there will be a quiz on the film, Joe continues to daydream. You have noticed Joe's pattern of inattentiveness during media presentations. He says the films are always boring and don't have anything to do with English. What can you do?

A. *Teaching Strategies*

(1) In this situation, you need to carefully examine the criticism received from Joe. If films are being shown too much, then a wider variety of materials should be presented. It may be that Joe's criticism is justified. Just changing an old routine at times will alleviate inattentiveness and boredom.

(2) Rather than watching films on a regular basis, students at this age enjoy interacting with one another. Providing peer interaction should be an integral part of instructional planning. For example, if the English topic is on writing good stories, a "round robin" game would be fun and would enhance the opportunity for interaction. To play this game, a topic would be provided by the teacher, and then the teacher would go around the room and have students make up supportive sentences. The end result is a class story that can be a permanent addition to the classroom.

(3) Prior to the beginning of each lesson, it is important for you to tie in the relevance of each assignment to the real world. In English, this is particularly important in the upper grades as many students do not see the need for learning such skills as conjugating verbs, reading what they consider outdated literary works, and improving their writing skills.

(4) Rather than a film-test approach, an alternative strategy might be to provide Joe with a set of questions about the film prior to its viewing and have him answer the questions during the film. This strategy would require that Joe focus more attention throughout the film.

(5) If the films are a central part of the curriculum, and in your judgment are essential for the rest of the class, an alternative strategy might be to have Joe complete an alternative study on the topic. For example, if a series of films of Shakespeare's plays are being shown in the class, you might contract with Joe and have him read the play independently and then have him make a game about the play for the class. For instance, Joe could make a bingo game in which the names of the characters or significant events of the play are recorded on bingo cards. Joe then can write questions about the characters or significant events to be used by the caller in the bingo game. This alternative strategy requires that Joe has read and

comprehended the play and also involves him in class participation. Additionally, if Joe is artistic, allowing him to create scenes of the play in some other medium might be an alternative strategy.

(6) If Joe's behavior is related to more general attention problems, providing Joe with alternative assignments would be more appropriate. Requiring Joe to sit through a lengthy film may be beyond his current capabilities. Assigning short tasks that provide for periodic breaks would increase the likelihood of success. For example, suppose the English topic is reviewing the parts of speech. Rather than having Joe watch the film, you might require that he complete a short worksheet on the topic, break briefly, then complete a self-checking poster activity on the topic.

(7) If Joe truly does not see the relevance of the films, have him make a list of activities that he believes would be more appropriate. Contracting with Joe to allow him to complete activities in a manner he sees as relevant would empower him with the responsibility for his own work.

B. Behavior Management Techniques

(1) Because Joe is a junior high or middle school student, it is important that you not single him out for strong punitive measures. Otherwise, you set the stage for "power" struggles with your students. Unless this problem is chronic and is costing Joe significantly, an appropriate consequence would be to allow Joe to assume responsibility for his own decision, particularly if Joe's behavior is related more to moodiness and an ill-tempered frame of mind. Allowing students at this age to learn "cause-and-effect" relations for their own choices teaches them responsibility.

(2) A reward system based on the principle of successive approximations might be beneficial. Reinforcing Joe for at-

tending for progressively longer periods of time over the course of several films might prove helpful. An appropriate reward for Joe would need to be determined ahead of time and a contract written. This contract would specify the minimal amount of time required at the onset of the system and also would need to specify the increments by which attending should increase per film.

6.6 Challenge: Grade 11

James is a quiet student in your U.S. History class who is making failing grades. He seldom turns in assignments, but when he does, you can tell he has the ability to do the work. James seldom interacts either with you or with his peers. You often forget to ask him questions or his opinions. In fact, you realize that you have overlooked him and spent a great deal of your time addressing the needs of students who seek your attention. Today, you pulled James aside and spoke to him about his failing grades. In response, James just shrugged his shoulders and offered you little insight into his lack of response.

A. *Teaching Strategies*

(1) Organize your lessons to incorporate small group activities/assignments. Assignments might be built upon the necessity of participation from each group member. For example, you might assign a project to each group, and each group member would be responsible for a certain portion of that assignment. Allow group members to interact and provide them with feedback and assistance when needed. Make sure James is assigned to a group of peers who are well adept socially so that he can model their behavior.

(2) Typically, withdrawn or shy students do not like to be called upon in class and are not likely to readily accept

your attention when lavished in front of a group. With James, a beginning step might be to arrange for him to work with you on an individual basis, perhaps during planning period or before homeroom. This first step should not focus on academics but should be a time for rapport building. For instance, get James involved in helping you with routine chores you have around the classroom or helping you complete a project that you are doing for the school. During this quiet time, get to know James but allow him to offer information to you as much as possible. Once a relationship is established, then a change in focus might be possible (e.g., calling on him in class when you are sure he knows the answer).

(3) During independent assignments, quietly check with James to see whether he needs your assistance. Offer suggestions when you see him on task.

(4) By talking to James, find a topic or subject of interest to him. Try to incorporate his topic into your planning by allowing him to do an independent study in lieu of his current assignments. For instance, if James is fond of horses, have him research the history of horses in our country. By contracting with James, he could complete a project on the essential role they have played in our country's history.

B. *Behavior Management Techniques*

(1) Talk with James and develop a contract for a passing grade in your course. Between the two of you, come up with assignments upon which you can both agree. Although these assignments may differ from what you expect of other students, it provides James with an opportunity to take responsibility for his grades and puts him on a path to passing your class. Additionally, by keeping track of his contractual requirements, you have developed a built-in system for giving him your attention.

7

Strategies for Collaboration

In this final chapter, we will discuss strategies in which teachers interact to share problems and develop plans to address identified problems. Such strategies are critically important because they (a) provide a support system for teachers, (b) provide a means for teachers to address concerns before they become more serious, (c) provide a means for teachers to get ideas on ways to meet the needs of students with identified disabilities within the mainstream, and (d) facilitate teachers becoming more prominent in the resolution and development of plans to address the needs of students experiencing mild learning and behavior problems.

7.1 What Are Ways Regular Classroom Teachers Can Work With Other Classroom Teachers to Solve Problems?

A. *Peer Collaboration*

This is a process that pairs regular classroom teachers to work together to solve classroom problems. Teachers use a programmed problem-solving process to develop a plan to address the needs of students experiencing learning and behavior problems. The four steps in the process are (a) problem identification and clarification of questions, (b) problem statement, (c) intervention identification, and (d) intervention evaluation. Pairs of teachers are taught to facilitate their partners' thinking and to guide them through the steps. When one of the pairs is experiencing a problem, one partner facilitates his or her thinking in a structured way through the four steps in the process. It has been reported that 85% of the problems brought to peer collaboration sessions end up with a resolution. Teachers using the process became more tolerant of diversity in student cognitive abilities and became more confident in successfully handling classroom problems. Finally, teachers using the process had significantly fewer referrals to special education than in previous years and fewer than their colleagues who did not use the process (Johnson & Pugach, 1991).

B. *Teacher Assistance Teams*

This is a process that has gained widespread application and a variety of names and hybrids. Some examples of variations are building support teams, intervention assistance teams, mainstreaming assistance teams, prereferral planning teams, teacher support teams, and so on. We can trace the conception of almost all these approaches back to Chalfant, Pysh, and Moultrie's (1979) original description of teacher assistance teams. In this approach, a group of teachers meet and brainstorm options for a teacher experiencing a classroom problem. Often effective teams can provide the support to enable teachers to address the needs of students experiencing mild behavior and learning problems. This system is very effective as long as it remains a teacher-driven support session. If it becomes a bureaucratic handle that one must get past to make a referral to special education, the process will lose impact (Pugach & Johnson, 1989).

C. Peer Coaching

This is a process in which teachers are paired or put into small groups to provide feedback to each other on teaching strategies. Coaches observe fellow teachers and help them target areas for enhancement and growth. The coach then continues observations to provide the teacher with feedback on progress toward identified goals. All teachers within the group can take turns functioning as the coach, or the most experienced or master teachers within the school can serve in this capacity.

D. Team Teaching

An effective way to maximize teacher strengths and minimize teacher weaknesses is to employ a team teaching approach. In such an approach, teachers are assigned to teach together and their classes are combined. Frequently, classes at different levels are combined such as kindergarten with first grade, first grade with second, second with third, and so on. This type of approach offers several advantages. First, the skills of two teachers can be combined to offset weaknesses. Second, there often are more opportunities for one of the teachers to work with individual students. Third, multiple-grade classes provide many occasions to include students in group activities appropriate for their abilities.

E. *Teacher Mentors*

There are formal and informal structures in which teacher mentors operate. Leaders naturally emerge in schools and can be a powerful source of professional growth for other teachers. Some schools have instituted formal structures to help beginning teachers make a successful transition into the profession. In these schools, master teachers are assigned to a new teacher to provide him or her with support and information to help create a successful transition. For a mentoring system to work, mentors must have the following characteristics:

(a) a supportive demeanor and the ability to facilitate the thinking of the beginning teacher,
(b) the ability to take a genuine interest in the beginning teacher,
(c) knowledge of when to intervene and when to back off and let the beginning teacher struggle with a problem, and
(d) the professional attributes of an accomplished master teacher.

7.2 Are There Ways Specialists in the School Can Support Classroom Teachers?

A. *Consultation*

One of the most important ways to support classroom teachers is through consultation. In this process, the special educator works with the classroom teacher to identify problems and develop solutions to those problems (Friend, 1988). This process typically has three steps:

(1) Problem identification. The consultant works with the classroom teacher to identify a problem. Typically, this includes

observations in the teacher's classroom and a series of discussions about what the problem is and factors that contribute to the problem.

(2) Strategy development. Based on the identified problem, a series of potential strategies are generated to solve the problem. The consultant and the consultee then jointly discuss the pros and cons of each strategy. The consultee eventually selects a strategy and then works with the consultant to develop an implementation plan that includes the following:

(a) a clear description of the problem,
(b) a clear description of the strategy to address the problem,
(c) a time when the strategy will be implemented,
(d) a procedure for how progress will be monitored,
(e) a plan for how problem resolution or the success of the strategy is to be determined, and
(f) a future date for a follow-up meeting or review meeting to be scheduled.

(3) Strategy implementation. The consultee proceeds with the plan as indicated in the implementation plan. If, at the review meeting, the plan is found to be unsatisfactory, each step in the process is reexamined and a new problem and/or implementation plan is developed.

7.3 Are There Barriers That Can Inhibit the Potential of Consultation to Enable Classroom Teachers to Solve Problems?

The successful implementation of consultation on the surface appears simple, but it is actually extremely complex (Johnson, Pugach, & Hammitte, 1988). If the consultant and consultee do not have a complete understanding of the process, it is likely to be unsuccessful and not a useful tool to solve problems. Continued training on the process is critical to supporting the process and avoiding barriers. The following are a series of common barriers with suggestions on how to avoid them.

A. *Strategy Incongruence*

There can be incongruence between the views of regular and special educators regarding appropriate and acceptable strategies to solve problems. For example, the orientation of special educators is often slanted toward individualized approaches that rely heavily on applied behavioral procedures, which is a different orientation than that of regular educators. Furthermore, the experiences of special educators with the problems of large group instruction are limited. As a result, there is an increased danger of strategies being suggested that are either unrealistic or outside the expertise of the regular classroom teacher. To avoid this problem, the consultant must value and practice good listening skills and be committed to facilitating greater understanding of the problem in the teacher's terms.

B. *Giving Advice*

Often there is an expectation, internal, external, or both, that consultants should be in control of the situation. Consultants may feel that they are ultimately responsible for the direction and outcome of the consultation. When such a situation occurs, the consultant may end up giving the consultee advice, either in response to the consultee's requests or because he or she is reluctant to engage in collaborative problem solving. Giving advice on a frequent basis is a dangerous trap that is destined to lead the consultation to failure. If the advice is successful, it can lead to dependency and inhibit the ability of the regular classroom teacher to engage in independent problem solving. Providing advice also frequently can lead to suggested strategies that the teacher is unable or unwilling to implement.

To avoid the advice trap, the consultant must recognize that the development of strategies and the selection of strategies is the responsibility of the classroom teacher. The primary role of the consultant is to help the teacher gain greater understanding and to be a sounding board for the pros and cons of potential strategies.

c. *Credibility Conflicts*

For consultation to be successful, participants must be credible in each other's eyes. Without such credibility, it is very unlikely that a successful resolution will result from the consultation. The literature suggests that there can be dissonance between the expectations of general and special educators regarding each other's expertise to address the needs of students with learning and behavior problems in the regular classroom (i.e., Aloia & Aloia, 1982; Furey & Strauch, 1983; Johnson & Johnson, 1980; Leyser & Abrams, 1984; Ringlaben & Price, 1981; Spodek, 1982). For example, if a regular classroom educator believes the suggestions made by the consultant to be unrealistic and/or if the consultant questions the commitment of the regular educator to make changes to address the needs of a specific student, the ability of these individuals to engage in a consultation to solve problems is nonexistent.

It takes time to develop credibility. A process in which all educators attend training meetings on the process and work together to develop the consultation option within the school can be the basis of the respect needed to ensure credibility. A second way to develop the respect of classroom teachers is for consultants to refrain from making judgments and to value the expertise of the classroom teacher by recognizing that it is the teacher's primary role to develop and select the strategy to address the identified problem.

D. *Confused Problem Ownership*

It is critical for both the consultant and the classroom teacher to recognize that the problem to be solved resides with the classroom teacher. As has already been discussed, the solution also resides with the classroom teacher. Therefore the consequences, either negative or positive for resolving or not resolving the problem, are primarily those of the classroom teacher. When consultants take on more responsibility than the regular classroom teacher in identifying problems and developing strategy implementation plans, the ownership of the problem can shift to the consultant. Once this occurs, the teacher's commitment to solve the problem can be diminished. The consultant may feel compelled to generate more and more ideas to help solve the problem as each previous suggestion fails. When such a shift occurs, it's not uncommon for teachers to confront a consultation with a statement like the following: "I tried spending five extra minutes each day going over assignments with Jody and she's still not doing her work. What are you going to do now?!" Once the teacher has become disengaged from the problem, it is unlikely that the problem will be solved.

As with the previous approaches to avoiding barriers, the behavior of the consultant can make a great contribution. The consultant should strive to facilitate thinking on the part of the classroom teacher and should continuously return the thinking of the classroom teacher back to the teacher him- or herself. The consultant also must be patient and allow the time needed by a classroom teacher to fully understand the problem and to develop a plan to address the problem. Pugach and Johnson (1989) demonstrated that, when teachers identify a problem and then spend time reflecting upon and discussing the problem, the original problem changes in more than 85% of the cases. Jumping too quickly to a plan to solve a problem before the problem has been adequately explored can lead to solutions for the wrong problem.

Key Terms

❏ *Consultation.* A specialist working with a regular classroom teacher to identify and solve classroom problems.

❏ *Peer coaching.* Teachers working together to improve teaching skills.

❏ *Peer collaboration.* A teacher-to-teacher process in which one individual facilitates his or her partner's problem solving.

❏ *Teacher assistance teams.* A group problem-solving process.

❏ *Teacher mentors.* Master teachers working with and supporting beginning teachers.

❏ *Team teaching.* Two teachers working together to teach their combined classes.

References

Aloia, G. F., & Aloia, S. D. (1983). Teacher expectation questionnaire. *Journal for Special Educators, 19*(2), 11-20.

Chalfant, J. C., Pysh, M., & Moultrie, P. (1979). Teacher assistance teams: A model for within-building problem solving. *Learning Disability Quarterly, 2,* 85-96.

Friend, M. (1988). Putting consultation into context: Historical and contemporary perspectives. *Remedial and Special Education, 9,* 7-13.

Furey, E. M., & Strauch, J. D. (1983). The perceptions of teachers skills and knowledge by regular and special educators of mildly handicapped students. *Teacher Education and Special Education, 6,* 46-50.

Johnson, D. W., & Johnson, R. T. (1980). Integrating handicapped students into the mainstream. *Exceptional Children, 47,* 90-99.

Johnson, L. J., & Pugach, M. C. (1991). Peer collaboration: Accommodating students with mild learning and behavior problems. *Exceptional Children, 58,* 454-461.

Johnson, L. J., Pugach, M. C., & Hammitte, D. J. (1988). Barriers to effective special education consultation. *Remedial and Special Education, 9,* 41-47.

Leyser, Y., & Abrams, P. D. (1984). Changing attitudes of classroom teachers toward mainstreaming through inservice training. *The Clearing House, 57,* 250-255.

Pugach, M. C., & Johnson, L. J. (1989). Prereferral interventions: Progress, problems, and challenges. *Exceptional Children, 56,* 217-226.

Ringlaben, R. P., & Price, J. (1981). Regular classroom teachers' perceptions of mainstreaming effects. *Exceptional Children, 47,* 302-304.

Spodek, B. (1982). What special educators need to know about regular classrooms. *The Educational Forum, 46,* 295-307.

Troubleshooting Guide

NOTES